Rain Forest
Coloring Book

ANNIKA BERNHARD

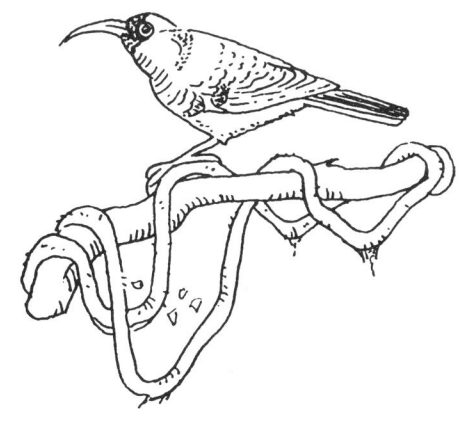

DOVER PUBLICATIONS, INC.
Mineola, New York

Bibliographical Note

Rain Forest Coloring Book is a new work, first published by Dover Publications, Inc., in 1998.

DOVER *Pictorial Archive* SERIES

International Standard Book Number: 0-486-40112-X

Manufactured in the United States of America
Dover Publications, Inc., 31 East 2nd Street, Mineola, N.Y. 11501

PUBLISHER'S NOTE

Scientists have identified dozens of different types of lowland and mountain rain forest, but for most people "rain forest" means a tropical rain forest. These are evergreen forests in the zone between the equator and the tropics of Cancer and Capricorn. They receive between 160 and 400 inches of rainfall annually and have an average temperature of about 80° F., with no significant cool or dry spells. Two-thirds of the world's rapidly disappearing rain forest is this tropical variety, extremely rich in both the diversity and quantity of its plant and animal life. The largest remnants of tropical rain forest are found in the basin of the Amazon River in South America, in the basin of the Congo River in Africa, along the east side of the large island of Madagascar off the coast of East Africa, and on the peninsula and islands of Malaysia in Southeast Asia, as well as on Borneo and other large islands that make up Indonesia. Tropical semi-deciduous forests—which are less rich in species because they receive less rainfall, have a lower average temperature, and experience an annual dry spell—are found in Burma, Cambodia, Thailand and Vietnam in Southeast Asia, on other

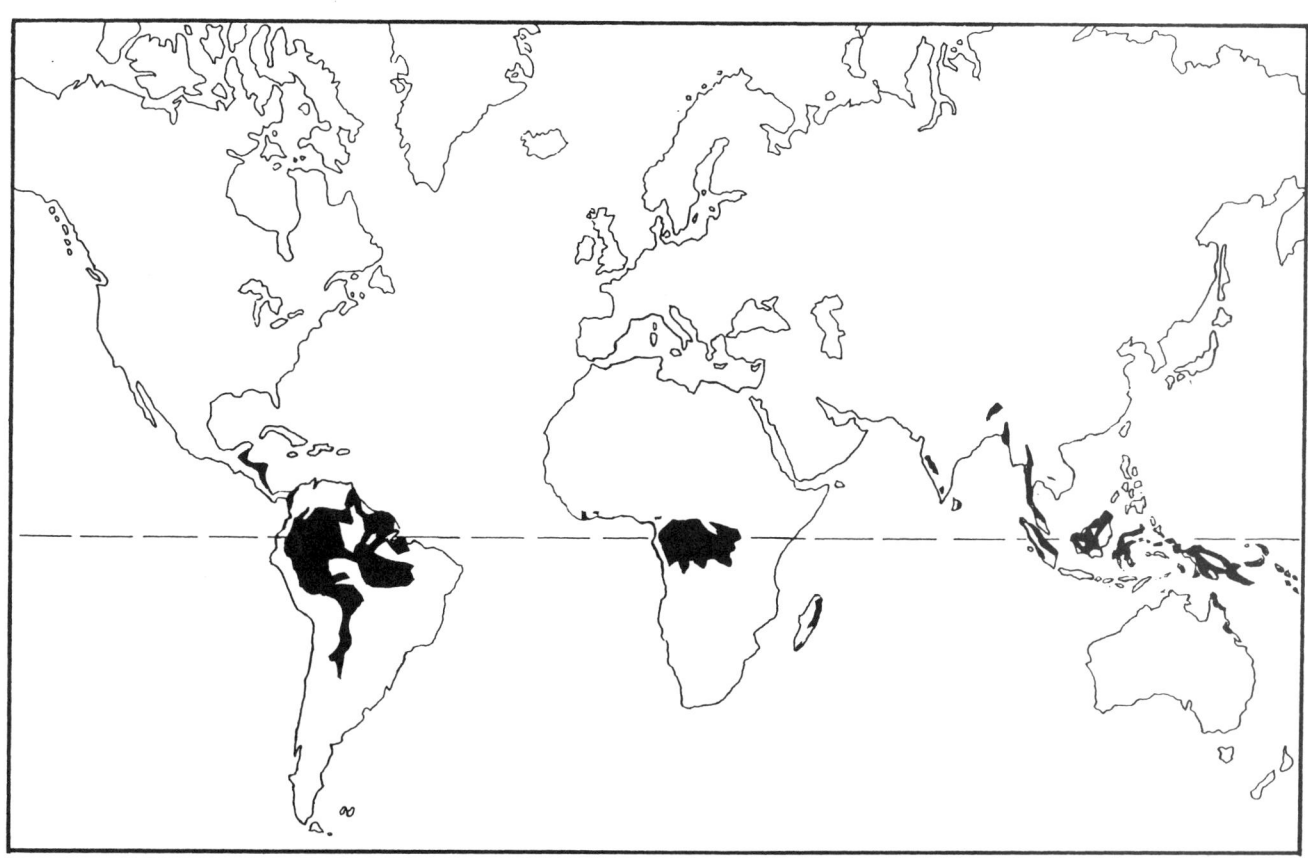

Indonesian islands, in the Philippines, in northeastern Australia, and in parts of West Africa, South America, and Central America. In the United States, small patches of rain forest exist on the islands of the state of Hawaii and in Puerto Rico and the U.S. Virgin Islands in the Caribbean.

It does not seem odd that rain forests would be common in wet tropical regions, but most people are surprised to learn that tropical rain forests covered much of the earth for millions of years—even as recently as 5 million years ago. (Scientists have found fossilized pollen grains of tropical rain forest species in London and in the states of Tennessee and Alaska in the United States.) About 20 million years ago, changes in the earth's climate and in the location of its land masses caused the rain forests to shrink to a band in the tropical zone, but rain forests still covered about 14 percent of the earth's land a few thousand years ago. In fact, not until after 1500 A.D. did increasingly aggressive exploration and exploitation of the world's continents and islands by Europeans result in the devastation of natural environments and the extinction of many species.

This destruction accelerated with the consumption of natural resources to fuel the Industrial Revolution, and multiplied again after World War II. Despite the many voices raised in the last quarter of the twentieth century, warning that rain forests must be preserved for human life on earth to remain possible, these irreplaceable resource treasuries were squandered at ever-faster rates. By the mid-1980s, only about 7 percent of the planet's land surface remained covered with rain forest, and most of that now is gone.

Christopher Columbus's 1492 description of the forests of a Caribbean island, Hispaniola, was the first European written account of a rain forest. The name "tropical rain forest" was not used until 1898, by a German botanist. Since then, much has been learned from study of species found in the rain forests. Currently, more than half of all drugs manufactured are based on plant substances, many of them found only in rain forests. Many potentially healing medications have been lost because of rain forest species becoming extinct without ever being discovered. From rain forest products, scientists have developed an array of substances useful in food, clothing, shelter, and technology. Still, what is known about tropical rain forests is only a tiny percentage of what is *not* known. Annual funding worldwide for all tropical biological research is only a few million dollars, while the United States alone spends several *billion* on space exploration. A way of saving the crucial biological diversity of species that live in rain forests (on which human life may depend), while enabling economic use of rain forest products, is the establishment of "extractive reserves" from which fruits, nuts, flowers, seeds, gums, resins, and other renewable resources can be harvested without destruction of the forests.

In the following pages, rain forest mammals, reptiles, amphibians, birds, insects, and fish found on four continents and on widespread islands are seen among the trees, flowers, ferns, lianas, and rivers where they have interdependently developed unique adaptations to their intricate environmental niches. Among them are many creatures remarkable for their large size, speed of growth, long lifespan, or unusual modes of camouflage, imitation, threat, attraction, or gaining nourishment. Many of the animal species depicted are in danger of extinction, because of habitat destruction and hunting. In some cases only a few survivors remain, in isolated habitats.

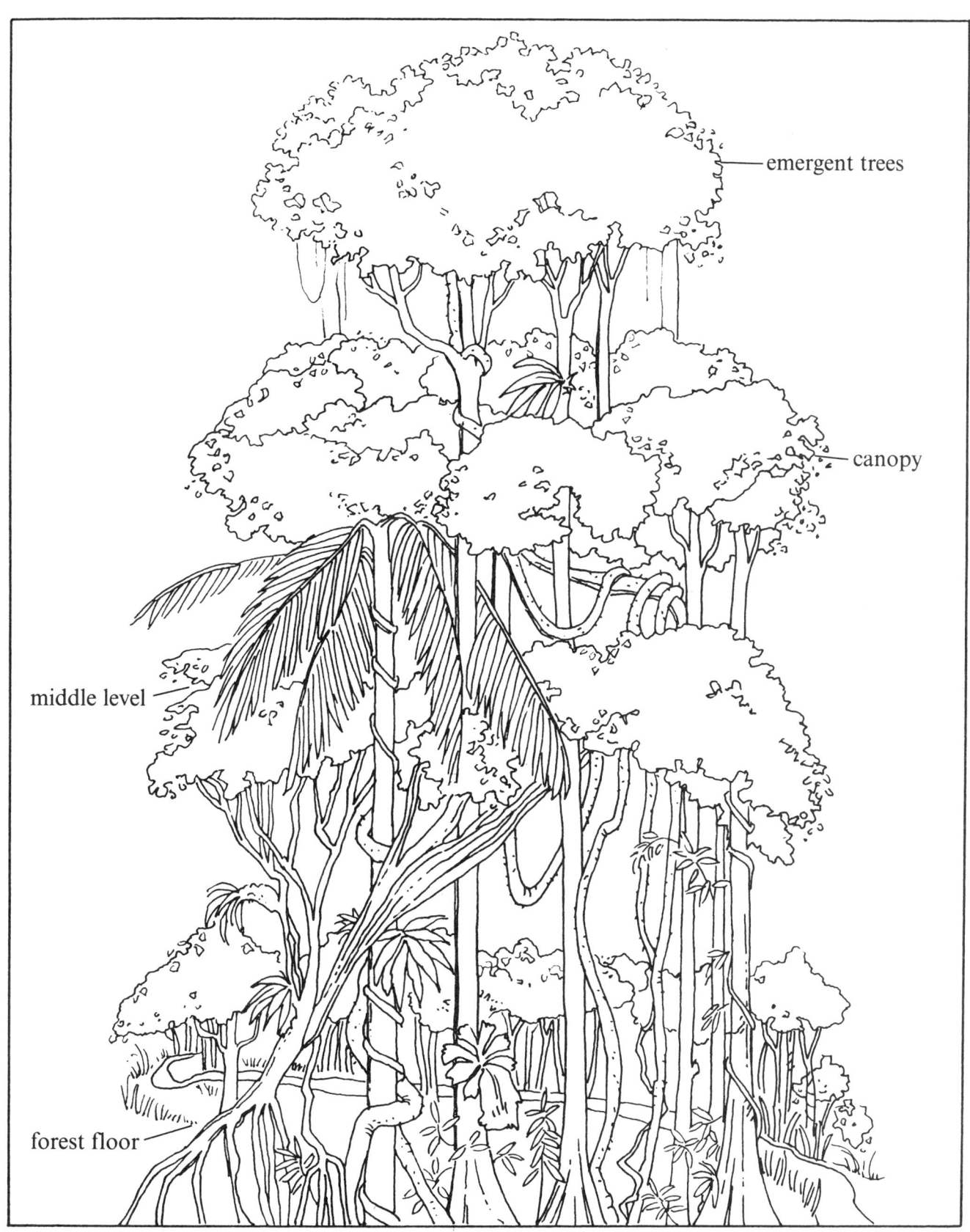

emergent trees

canopy

middle level

forest floor

Rain forests have five distinct levels or layers: the emergent trees that protrude above the lower levels; the canopy formed by the crowns of other tall trees; the middle level of shorter trees; the understory composed of shrubs, herbs, vines, and other low-growing plants; and the forest floor, which is covered with a thick layer of decomposing matter. A tropical rain forest recycles nutrients so efficiently that hardly any are wasted. Some rain forest animals spend their entire lives in the canopy or on the forest floor; others freely move between levels.

5

In the forests of west central Africa, the **crowned hawk eagle** *(Stephanosetus coronatus)* nests in emergent trees and swoops down on monkeys, its main food. The **mandrill** *(Papio sphynx),* at right, has a memorable face, with a bright-red snout and flat blue-and-white areas on its cheeks. The **collared sunbird** *(Anthreptes collaris),* at right, pollinates bright-colored, odorless flowers as it drinks their nectar, while the **yellow-casqued hornbill** *(Ceratogymna elata),* at left, prefers a diet of grasshoppers. Deforestation has endangered the **western black-and-white colobus monkey** *(Colobus polykomos),* at left, which eats leaves as well as fruit.

The **Cuvier toucan** (*Ramphastos cuvieri*) of South America bears the brightly colored, large but lightweight beak typical of toucans (it has a honeycomb structure). The **postman butterfly** (*Heliconius melpomene*), like many related species, warns predators by its gaudy wing colors that its body contains noxious juices. Caterpillars of some *Heliconius* species may ingest poisonous chemicals while feeding on *Passiflora* species (*Passiflora caerulea,* the **blue passionflower,** which has blue, white, and purple bands on the corona, is shown here), thus becoming poisonous themselves. A Roman Catholic tradition maintains that the various parts of the passionflower symbolize elements of the crucifixion of Christ.

The rare **harpy eagle** *(Harpia harpyja)* of South America can fly through the canopy at fifty miles per hour, seizing monkeys in its huge talons. The world's largest raptor (meat-eating bird), it weighs up to 20 pounds and has a six-foot wingspan. **Queen Alexandra's birdwing** *(Ornothoptera alexandrae)* is the largest known butterfly. As a caterpillar, it has fleshy, pointed red ten-tacles on a black body. The upper surface of the male's wings is blue, black, green, and yellow, the rear portion of the body bright yellow. The **eyelash viper** *(Bothriechis/Bothrops schlegeli)* is named for the spiny scales above its eyes. Its body usually is yellow, with white, black, or red spots. A night hunter, it captures tree frogs, often eating them while hanging by its tail.

The **brown-throated three-toed sloth** *(Bradypus variegatus)* likes to feed on leaves of the **trumpet tree** *(Cecropia peltata)*, which often grows on riverbanks. Hollow nodes in the tree's trunk and branches are home to **Aztec ants** *(Azteca* species), which protect it from the ravages of leaf-cutter ants while feeding on growths called Müllerian bodies. The tree growths contain glycogen, a starch usually produced only by animals. The sloth's gray-brown fur appears to have a green tinge because algae grow in it. Hundreds of insects live in a sloth's fur, too. Unlike most mammals, the sloth cannot maintain a steady body temperature; it hangs in sunny spots to absorb heat. A lethargic creature, it crawls when on the ground, but swims well and can plummet into a river to escape attack.

9

The female Central American **tree frog** (*Hemiphractus* species) carries her eggs in a depression on her back. These tree frogs have bony, triangular heads and long, pointed snouts. The tadpoles often live in the water that collects at the base of the leaves of bromeliads (called "tank plants" or "urn plants"). These frogs do not vocalize. The **imperial parrot** (*Amazona imperialis*) has a dark-green upper body, multicolored plumage below with a purple sheen overall, and a reddish-brown tail with a pink tip. Its habitat has been destroyed almost entirely, by Caribbean hurricanes and by forest clearance. It lays only two eggs when it nests. At the lower right is a **hunting wasp**, a member of the Vespidae family.

The **emerald tree boa** (*Corallus canina*) in its adult stage is emerald green with white bands and flecks. Sensitive heat receptors around its lips (near the large fangs) help it locate its prey. **Morpho butterflies** (*Morpho* species) have been called "the bluest thing in the world" because of the striking, iridescent upper surface of the males' wings. Each pair of wings consists of an estimated 1.5 million tiny scales; only about 20 percent of them appear blue when seen through a microscope. The wings' undersides have protective coloration and glaring eyespots. The **buff saki** (*Pithecia albicans*) has a mostly black back and tail, but otherwise varies in color from buff to reddish. Active by day, it lives in trees, which it descends tail first.

The **bee hummingbird** *(Mellisuga hellenae),* at top, is the smallest living bird, 2 1/4 inches from beak tip to tail tip, with a maximum wingspan of 4 inches. Its eggs weigh about 5/1000 ounce. The **brown violet-eared hummingbird** *(Colibri delphinae),* found from northern Central America to Brazil, is closely related to green, sparkling, and white-vented varieties. All hummingbirds eat insects and drink nectar from flowers, pollinating as they go. They "hibernate" at night, saving energy with vastly slowed heartbeat and breathing, because they maintain incredibly rapid wingbeats while flying and hovering during the day. The **white-tipped sicklebill** *(Eutoxeres aquila)* is found from southern Central America to Peru.

The **squirrel monkey** *(Saimiri sciurea),* a short-haired, very active monkey with a prehensile tail, lives in troops of a dozen to more than thirty animals. The **red-eyed tree frog** *(Agalychnis callidryas)* is nocturnal and slow-moving. It has adhesive pads on its fingers and toes, and can grip objects between its thumb and other fingers. Tadpoles hatch in about six days and often live within the water tank of a bromeliad—a member of the Bromeliaceae family, to which the pineapple plant belongs. Unlike pineapple plants, the bromeliads pictured here *(Vriesea heterostachus)* are epiphytes ("air plants" that grow without having roots in soil).

The cloud forest (rain forest on mountain slopes where clouds gather) is a misty world all morning and remains very moist when the afternoon sun shines on it. The **golden toad** *(Bufo periglenes),* discovered in 1963, by the mid-1980s was found only in the tiny Monte Verde forest reserve in Costa Rica, Central America. No golden toads have been seen since 1989. The species' name refers to the male's vivid orange color; females are olive-green or black with crimson spots. These toads usually mate in water. Eggs expelled by the female are fertilized outside her body. Epiphytes (center and right foreground) grow on tree branches and trunks without getting nutrients through roots in the soil. The approximately sixty *Cattleya* species of orchids found in tropical America are epiphytes ("air plants").

The **common** or **green iguana** *(Iguana iguana)* reaches six feet in length and lives in trees. The young eat insects, but adults prefer buds. Iguanas can escape predators such as hawks and boas by jumping as much as fifty feet to the ground or swimming underwater. This species of **poison-dart frog** *(Dendrobates leucomelus)* is bright red and black. It lives in leaf litter or in epiphytic bromeliads high in trees. The various *Dendrobates* frogs are unaggressive, but tribal hunters in the Amazon River region kill them while extracting a powerful poison from skin glands. They use the poison on their darts. Diverse orchid species grow in tropical rain forests as epiphytes ("air plants"). This species *(Cattleya forbesii)* has yellow-green flowers with white or yellow edges and is popular for corsages.

15

The **howler monkey** *(Alouatta species)*, at top, is the largest American monkey, with a two-foot tail equal in length to its head and body. The male especially has a large larynx, and produces a call at dawn and dusk that can be heard for two miles through the forest. The **spider monkey** *(Ateles paniscus)* lives near the forest edge. A sloppy eater, it drops a lot of fruit, thus dispersing the seeds from which new trees grow. The thorny-branched **cannonball tree** *(Couroupita guianensis)* is named for its round fruit, about eight inches in diameter, which has a red-brown, woody shell. Loud crashes are heard when the fruit falls to the ground. The flesh inside the shell has an unpleasant odor.

Like all mantises, the **orchid mantis** (*Hymenopus coronatus*), seen in the foreground, differs from other insects in that it can turn its head considerably, because it has a flexible neck. This species is more remarkable for its resemblance to a pink orchid that grows in the rain forests of Malaysia. The insect's fringed wings help it to camouflage itself as a flower. It is said to do this so well that it attracts butterflies seeking flower nectar. The mantis then grasps the butterflies between its forelegs and eats them. Several mantis species in Malaysia and Indonesia imitate flowers. The mantis seen in the background is a *Polyspilota* species found in Africa. It is green and brown, like the praying mantis native to Europe. The female mantis is notorious for eating the male after mating.

Buffon's macaw *(Ara ambigua),* found from Central America to Ecuador in South America, is the largest of the macaws, which are members of the parrot family. Many have been killed to obtain their tail feathers, which are used to make headdresses worn by folk dancers who perform for tourists. The common fig tree represented fertility, joy, and the afterlife to the ancient Egyptians. The **strangler fig** *(Ficus aurea)* usually begins life when an animal drops a seed on a tree branch. The seed sends roots down to the forest floor. The roots spread, caging the host tree. Eventually (it may take a hundred years) the other tree dies, smothered by the fig tree, which can produce 100,000 fruits at one time. The flowers (lower right) are of *Guzmania lingulata,* a bromeliad. Water collects in the "tank" formed at the base of bromeliads' stiff leaves.

18

The slow-moving **potto** *(Perodicticus potto)* lives in west central Africa. This thick-furred creature weighs about three pounds. It sleeps in trees during the day and is active at night. The potto has strong hands and feet. It butts adversaries in the eyes and nose with its sharp, protruding neck vertebrae. Pottos feed on fruit as well as insects and their larvae. The **calabash nutmeg** *(Monodora myristica),* also known as the African nutmeg, is a tall tree with long, drooping leaves. The aromatic seeds of the hard-shelled fruit are used as a spice, like the more familiar nutmeg that originated in the Molucca islands of Indonesia.

The **flying gecko** or **fringed gecko** (*Ptychozoon kuhli*), at right, can "parachute" more than thirty feet, aided by fleshy flaps along its sides and by webbed toes. Geckos, active at night, have eyes with vertical-slit pupils like those of cats. The **flap-necked chameleon** (*Chamaeleo dilepis*) coils the end of its tail around branches. It catches insect prey by shooting out its very long tongue, which is tipped with a bell-shaped suction cap. Each eye has a separate field of vision, so it can watch its next meal and look out for predators at the same time. The **Goliath beetle** (*Goliathus druryi*), lower left, is one of the largest and heaviest flying insects. Vine-like lianas cling to growing trees with tendrils and may extend for thousands of feet as they climb toward the sunlight.

The **great hornbill** (*Buceros bicornis*) lives in the lowlands of Southeast Asia, from India to the island of Sumatra in Indonesia. A sizable bird (52 inches long), it eats large insects, especially grasshoppers. Its plumage is black and white, but the casque (helmet) atop its head is yellow, as is its beak, which is red at the tip and orange in the middle. Young hornbills take a relatively long time to learn to fly—as much as eight weeks. The **red silk-cotton tree** (*Bombax ceiba*) reaches a height of 75 feet. Its red flowers grow near the ends of the branches.

The **tree porcupine** *(Coendou prehensilis)* has a prehensile tail for gripping branches. Its short, barbed spines are not always readily visible among its fur. A nocturnal creature, it shelters in a burrow or a hollow log during the day. *Mandevilla splendens* is a vine with funnel-shaped, fragrant, vibrant-pink flowers. More than 2,700 species of **palm trees** exist.

The **kookaburra** *(Dacelo novaeguineae),* found in Australia and on the large island of New Guinea to the north, is also called the laughing jackass, because the sound it makes before dawn resembles human laughter. It is a member of the kingfisher family, but eats mice, snakes, other small animals, and large insects, rather than fish. The **red-flowering gum tree** *(Eucalyptus ficifolia),* one of about five hundred eucalyptus species native to Australia, got its Latin name because its leaves (foliage) resemble those of the species of fig tree *(Ficus)* that grows there. The leathery, dark-green leaves contrast with the tree's masses of red flowers. The *Alcidis metaurus* **moth** has blue-green bands on its black wings, which have a coppery sheen. It pollinates flowers as it sips nectar during the day.

The **ruffed lemur** *(Varecia variegata)* is active at night, unlike other lemurs. Its face and limbs are black, the chin hair and ear tufts are white, and the body is piebald. Lemur species exist only on the large island of Madagascar, east of Africa, where true monkeys never evolved. Scientists have observed six lemur species drinking flower nectar. Lemurs are the only mammals except tropical bats to do so. By carrying pollen on their fur, they spread plant species. The female ruffed lemur gives birth to twins. Small groups of ruffed lemurs can emit a roar heard more than half a mile away. The flowers of the **grapple plant** *(Umicarina grandidieri)* are yellow outside and deep purple inside. Its fruit (not shown) is protected by dangerous barbed spines.

As a caterpillar (at lower left), this **hawk moth** species can drive away predators by turning upside down, which makes one end of its body resemble the head of a poisonous snake (center). The caterpillar moves its body to imitate the movements of the snake's head. When the **hummingbird hawk moth** *(Macroglossum stellatarum)* hovers to take nectar from a flower (at upper right) with its three-inch-long tongue, it beats its wings backward and forward, with the upper surface of the wing turned downward during the backward strokes. Hawk moths *(Sphingidae)* visit flowers both by day and by night, using visual cues as well as scent to choose blossoms.

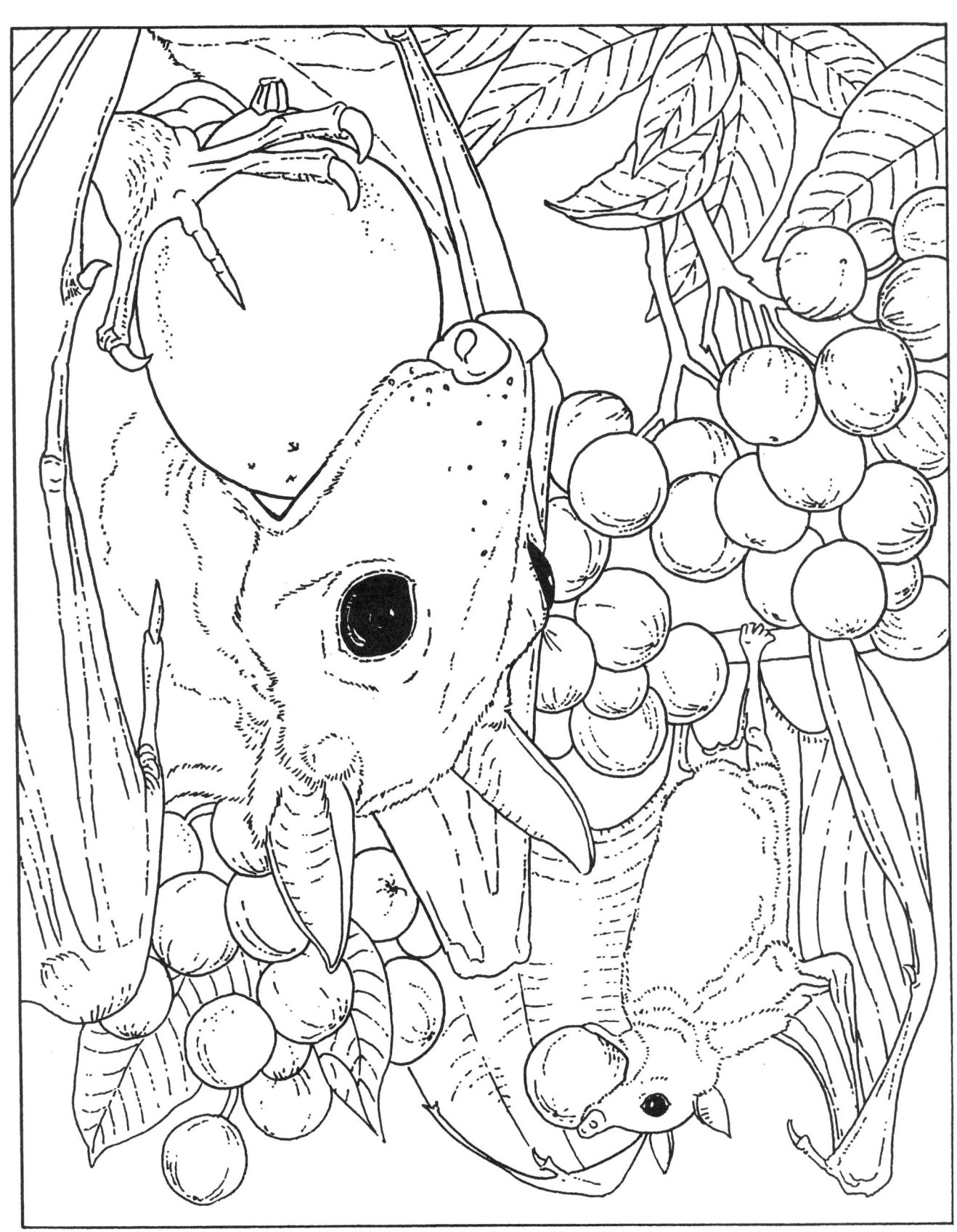

The **hammerhead bat** *(Hypsignathus monstrosus),* found in central Africa, is named for its remarkably horselike muzzle or snout, which has ample cheek pouches. Its larynx occupies a fifth of its body cavity. Adult males emit a "kwok" sound—reputedly every second, all night. The hammerhead bat is among the large, fruit-eating bats. A solitary creature, it does not live in colonies.

26

The **mudar** or **madar tree** *(Calotropis procera)* grows near the edges of African forests, near water. It usually is less than six feet tall, but can reach fifteen feet in height. Its inner bark yields a fiber used in making rope, and silky fibers that surround the seeds of its fruit are used as a substitute for kapok (a substance from Malaysian silk-cotton trees that provides buoyancy and insulation). The tree exudes a milky liquid that resembles gutta percha (a tough, elastic substance like rubber, but with more resin, extracted from some trees in Malaysia). Children in west central Africa sometimes play with the **Goliath beetle** *(Goliathus druryi),* which may be six inches long and weigh six ounces or more.

27

About seventy species of carnivorous "**pitcher plants**" exist. Insects attracted by the sweet juices of their leaves slide down the smooth, slippery sides of their deep, narrow "pitchers" and are digested by pepsin and other chemicals. Many pitcher plants grow as epiphytes, but some take root in the forest floor. *Nepenthes rafflesiana,* shown here, is found in Malaysia, on nearby Borneo, and on other islands in Indonesia. Its pitcher is pale green with purple veins, and may be ten inches tall, with a four-inch-wide opening at the top.

The **ring-tailed lemur** *(Lemur catta)* has pale gray and white fur on its body, black rings around its eyes, and a black-and-white ringed tail. It lives at the southern end of the island of Madagascar, eating fruit and young leaves. Unlike other lemurs, it spends more time on the ground than in trees. Males engage in stink fights. The common periwinkle was known to the French as the "sorcerer's violet" and to the Italians as "the flower of death," and in medieval England condemned men were forced to wear periwinkle garlands on their way to the gallows. However, extracts from the **Madagascar periwinkle** *(Catharanthus roseus)* prolong and enhance life, as medicines very effective in treating Hodgkin's disease and juvenile leukemia.

The **red piranha** (*Serrasalmus nattereri*) is one of five carnivorous species of large piranha (it can be a foot long). A fast swimmer with sharp, triangular teeth, it feeds on smaller fish as well as plant matter, and attacks animals or humans in shallow, muddy, agitated, or blood-stained water. If several are imprisoned together, these piranha will attack each other. One tribe in the Amazon River region uses piranha to clean the flesh from the skeletons of their dead. The **giant water lily** (*Victoria amazonica*) grows in seven months from a tiny seed to a plant with flowers 8 inches in diameter, leaves 6 feet in diameter, and stems 18 feet long. Each flower lives only two days. When pollinated (often by large beetles) flowers sink into the river, but the seeds float to the surface and are dispersed by the current.

The **chimpanzee** *(Pan troglodytes)* stands about three feet tall and has no tail. It is heavy and strong: an adult male may weigh 180 pounds. Chimpanzee vocalizations range from loud howls and screams to quiet whimpers and grunts. These intelligent, playful apes also use body posture, facial expressions, and gestures to communicate. Troops move about on the forest floor, mainly eating fruit and plant shoots. The **banana** plant *(Musa* species) is a giant herb, not a tree, and originated in Asia. Christopher Columbus brought it to America from the Canary Islands, off Africa's west coast, where the Portuguese had planted it. A false trunk grows from an underground rhizome (horizontal root). The banana plant dies after producing fruit.

The **ocelot** *(Felis pardalis)* is a relatively small predatory cat, from about two to three feet long, with a tail about half as long as its body, and weighs up to 35 pounds. A tree dweller, it usually hunts small animals and birds at night. It ranges in color from pale yellow to white to tawny to gray, with dark spots and stripes on its coat. The **flamingo flower** *(Anthurium andraeanum)*, an epiphyte that grows high in trees, has a red or scarlet "quilted" sheath, six to ten inches tall, for the flower cluster, which is a drooping, yellow, fleshy spike, and leathery leaves. When threatened, the **lantern bug** *(Fulgora lampetis)* spreads its wings, showing two large eyespots to frighten predators. At first sighting, its very long head was reported to be luminous, but this claim never has been proven.

The above-ground roots of the **stilt palm** grow downward, into the soil, in forest areas that are flooded frequently. The **scarlet ibis** *(Eudocimus ruber)* uses its long, down-curved black beak to seize shrimp, fish, and worms. It nests in tree tops. **Baird's tapir** *(Tapirus bairdii),* a vegetarian active mainly at night, can be six feet long and more than two feet tall at the shoulder. The large **Central American river turtle** *(Dermatemys mawii)* is endangered because its eggs and meat are considered delicacies. It forages on aquatic plants at the river bottom during the night and rarely leaves the water. The **giant otter** *(Pteronura brasiliensis)* is six feet long from nose to tail tip. It catches fish underwater and makes riverbank dens with submerged entrances.

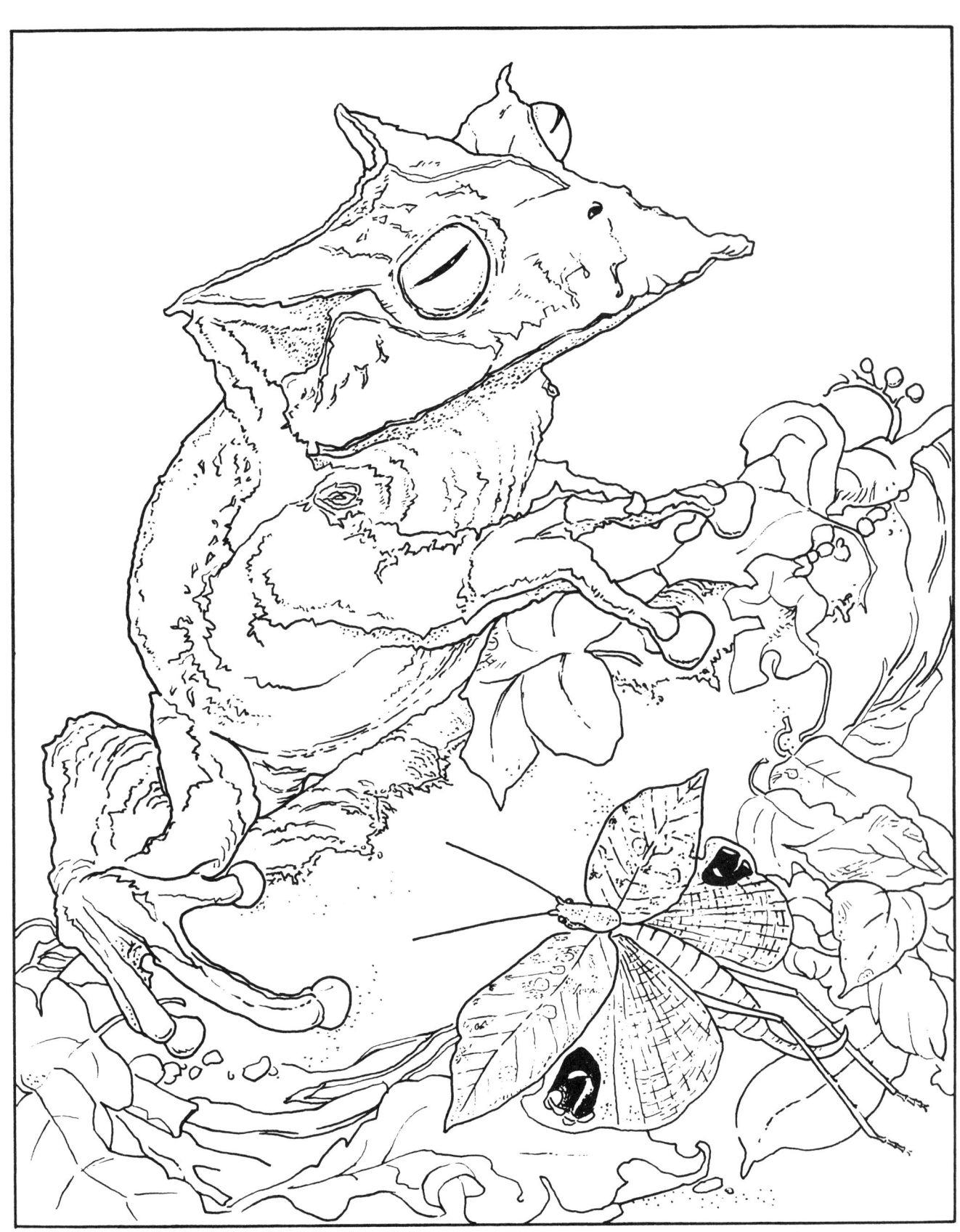

The **casque-headed frog** *(Hemiphractus proboscideus)*, found in Ecuador, lives on the forest floor, camouflaged as a dead leaf. Females carry their eggs on their backs. Tiny frogs hatch directly from the eggs, without first going through a tadpole stage. The **grasshopper** *(Ommatopia pictifolia)* blends with the leaf litter on the forest floor, but when startled spreads its wings, revealing a pair of large eyespots on the hind wings.

The **cassowary** *(Casuarius casuarius)* is a fierce, flightless bird that runs rapidly through the rain forest. It is native to north-eastern Australia, with a related species in New Guinea. Nearly six feet tall and weighing about 125 pounds, it has strong, sharp claws and is a powerful swimmer. Its head and neck feathers are bright blue and purple. Long red wattles and a large brown "helmet" complete its colorful head. The body feathers are black and waterproof. Cassowaries eat berries and fruit, and will toss a large fruit into the air, then swallow it whole. **Orchids** of the various *Dendrobium* species of Asia, Australia, and the Pacific islands grow profusely. As many as fifty different orchid species may be found on a single tree.

The **orangutan** *(Pongo pygmaeus)* is an orange or reddish-brown ape that lives in the forests of the islands of Sumatra (which is part of Indonesia) and Borneo. Active during the day, the orangutan moves through the forest alone, except that the young remain with their mother for five to six years. Orangutans prepare a new nest for each night. They range from four to five feet tall, and adult males weigh about 200 pounds. Fruit, plants, and animals are included in their diet. Epiphytic **orchids** of the numerous *Dendrobium* species are plentiful in the rain forests where orangutans dwell.

The **giant armadillo** *(Priodontes giganteus)* is three feet long, with a two-foot tail, and weighs 120 pounds. Its skin resembles hardened leather. Armadillos use scent to locate insects, then dig them from the ground with their clawed front feet. They are mammals, not reptiles: females nourish their young with milk, and they maintain a fairly steady body temperature. **Butterflies** of the many *Heliconius* species found in tropical America have long, slender forewings. They strongly prefer yellow pollen as food. Their caterpillars feed on the leaves of many passionflower vine species, but trichomes (short, barbed hairs) on the leaves of some passionflower plants discourage the butterflies from laying eggs there.

The **leaf-cutter ants** (39 *Atta* and *Acromyrmex* species) excavate huge underground nests. They live in colonies of about a million worker ants, founded by "queens" with an estimated lifespan of ten years. These ants maintain fungi "farms" on compost made by chewing up dime-sized bits of leaves. It has been calculated that 12-17 percent of all leaf surface in American rain forests is removed by leaf-cutter ants, which prefer young leaves. After a week of feeding on the colony's fungal food supply, worker ants emerge to harvest leaf bits. The **collared anteater** *(Tamandua tetradactyla)* is about two feet long and has a prehensile tail, similarly long, that is hairless on the underside. Its short, coarse fur is varicolored in bands and patches. Active at night, it lives both on the ground and in trees.

The **jaguar** *(Panthera onca)*, once common in Central America and northern South America, is now rare, and protected on only one reserve in Belize. A solitary, mainly nocturnal predator, about six feet long and weighing up to 125 pounds, it uses strong jaws, sharp teeth, and broad, clawed paws to kill armadillos, tapirs, anteaters, and other large mammals. The jaguar's fur is rusty yellow with black spots, and it has green eyes. *Mandevilla splendens* is a vine with rosy-pink, funnel-shaped flowers, which are pollinated by long-beaked birds that drink the ample nectar inside.

Dumb cane (*Dieffenbachia picta*) leaves have chemicals that cause pain and paralysis of the vocal chords when chewed. The leaves and stems also irritate the skin. The **spectacled caiman** (*Caiman crocodilus*) is named for a bony ridge on its head, between the eyes. It reaches eight feet in length and its average lifespan matches that of humans. Caimans, more closely related to alligators than to crocodiles, have bony plates beneath the skin of their underside and move very quickly in water and on land. The **boa** (*Boa constrictor*), up to eighteen feet long, mainly lurks in trees and hunts at night, suffocating its prey by tightening its coils so the victim's lungs can't expand. The many **hawk moth** species (Sphingidae family) are fast flyers, moving at up to 30 mph when not hovering to sip nectar.

The **butterfly** *(Amarynthis meneria meneria)* is an active pollinator of flowers. The **kingfisher** *(Alcedo* species) dives for fish from low branches overhanging water and makes its nest at the end of a long tunnel it excavates in the riverbank. Some kingfishers dig for worms (in New Guinea). Others catch land snails and smash their shells on stones (in the Philippines) or snap up flying termites (in Africa). Most of the more than five hundred *Eucalyptus* species are native to Australia and New Guinea, but many varieties of **eucalyptus** tree have been introduced to other parts of the world.

The **Bengal tiger** *(Panthera tigris tigris)* is ten feet long, from nose to tail tip. It is one of seven Asian tiger subspecies—all now very rare or extinct. One sanctuary in India protects the Bengal tiger, which preys on water buffalo and other grazing animals but will battle a python or a crocodile. *Rafflesia arnoldii* or *titan,* a parasitical plant, has the world's largest flowers—three feet wide, weighing fifteen pounds, with petals an inch thick. The plant's strong odor of decay attracts insects that feed on dead animals. The insects pollinate the flower. In 1818 a Malaysian guide showed the plant to naturalist Dr. Joseph Arnold, who was giving Sir Stamford Raffles and his wife a rain forest tour. *Lepeostegeres beccarii,* in the background, is a semiparasitic plant that produces green leaves, which means it does not get all its nutrients from the host plant.

The **aye-aye** *(Daubentonia madagascariensis)*, closely related to the lemurs of Madagascar, makes a "ha-hay" sound. Its fingers and toes all have claws, except the big toe. The aye-aye has dark-brown fur, with a paler face and large, mobile ears. It is solitary and feeds at night, using its rodent-like teeth to strip tree bark and its delicate third finger to extract insect grubs that live beneath it. It has been near extinction for decades; local people killed aye-ayes because they believed that the sight of one foretold a human death, and because the animals raid coconut plantations. The **dwarf glory lily** *(Gloriosa simplex)* is a climbing plant that clings to trees with tendrils that grow from its leaves. Its flowers are red or yellow.

The **hyacinthine macaw** (*Anodorhynchus hyacinthinus*), the largest member of the parrot family, has a bright blue head, golden yellow around the eyes and behind the lower beak, which is black and used for cracking nuts. It nests in large cavities in trees. Some ferns are as tall as trees, but ferns do not grow from seeds as trees do. Ferns reproduce by means of spores, which usually are on the undersides of their leaves. Epiphytic ferns grow on trees, with orchids. The **flumenense swallowtail** (*Parides ascanius*) is a butterfly that will not lay its eggs where others are. Some plants' leaves have small yellow bodies that resemble butterfly eggs. Butterflies don't deposit their eggs on those plants, which avoid having their leaves eaten by butterfly larvae or caterpillars.

An adult male **mountain gorilla** *(Gorilla gorilla beringei)* is about six feet tall, has an armspread of eight feet, and weighs up to 440 pounds. Females are about half that size. Because they are too heavy to climb trees, gorillas must find all their food on the forest floor. They are mainly vegetarian and feed during the day, living in troops of ten to twenty animals. They use their long arms as well as their legs in walking, putting their weight on their knuckles. **Bamboo** *(Arundinaria alpina)* is a treelike grass that grows in hollow, rigid woody segments. New shoots grow from underground stems. Bamboo has been known to grow forty inches in forty days.

45

This species of **archer fish** *(Toxotes jaculatrix)* is about seven inches long and lives near the surface in fresh water or in brackish water such as river estuaries. It uses a jet of water to shoot down insects that are up to twenty inches away. The **East Indies glass catfish** *(Kryptopterus macrocephalus)* is thin and yellow-green or gray in color, but has an iridescent blue tinge in sunlight. The **tiger barb** *(Puntius hexazona)* is found in Indonesia and Malaysia. **Mangroves** *(Rhizophora* species) are evergreen trees and shrubs adapted to seashores and marshes. Their spreading roots anchor them, while small, fingerlike roots that stick up through the mud allow them to "breathe."

Among the many tribes native to the rain forests of the world are the Yanomami, one of several groups of Amazon dwellers whose numbers have dwindled sharply in the twentieth century because of pollution and destruction of the environment (by gold mining, lumbering, and burning to "clear" land for pastures and crops) and because of the introduction of diseases to which they have no resistance. (Between 1989 and 1997, 21 percent of the Yanomami population died from such diseases, after a gold rush brought 45,000 miners to the area.) Their traditional way of life depends on hunting and gathering, which has sustained human groups in small numbers for thousands of years, as they harvest and use renewable plant and animal resources.

LIST OF COMMON NAMES

LIST OF SCIENTIFIC NAMES